usea his psychic gifts to track serial
killers, work for the FBI and the CIA.
He is the Mind-Power coach to
Premier League footballers,
industrialists, Formula One drivers
and racing cyclists. Honorary Vice-
President of Royal Berkshire Hospital,
close to his Thames-side home, he is
the father of two teenagers and the
author of eight best-sellers,
including the novel, *Ella*.

URI GELLER'S
LITTLE BOOK
OF MIND-POWER

*Maximise Your
Will to Win*

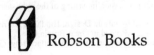

Robson Books

First published in Great Britain in 1998 by Robson Books Ltd,
Bolsover House, 5-6 Clipstone Street, London W1P 8LE

Designed by Harold King

British Library Cataloguing in Publication Data
A catalogue record for this title is available
from the British Library

ISBN 1 86105 193 X

Typeset by Pitfold Design, Hindhead, Surrey
Printed in Great Britain by
Caledonian International Book Manufacturing, Glasgow

'The longest journey of any person is the journey inward.'

Dag Hammerskjvld

'Whatever you can do or dream you can, begin it. Boldness has genius, power, and magic in it. Begin it now.'

Göethe

URI'S
TOP TEN STEPS
TO SUCCESS
Or . . .
Wake up your
willpower

◆

1
Write down exactly what
you want to achieve.
Word it clearly.
This is the **TARGET**.

◆

2
Repeat the **Target** over and over. Believe in it.

3
Forbid all other ideas to
distract you from the
Target.

4
Imagine how life will be when you achieve the **Target**. Picture and visualize the details vividly, with tastes, sensations and sounds.

5
Create a movie in your head and watch yourself achieving your aim – hitting the **Target**.

◆

6
Visualise how others will react to you when you have achieved your **Target**.

◆

7
Speak out clearly. Never mumble. How else can the world hear you?

8

Before you sleep, run the **Target** words three times through your mind, like a hypnotist.

9

Always believe in yourself. *You* have the Mind-Power.

10
Only you can achieve
your **Target**. No-one else
can do it for you. Seize
the responsibility.
Go for it!

'For all sad words of tongue
and pen, The saddest are these,
"It might have been".'

John Greenleaf Whittier

'Twenty years from now you will be
more disappointed by the things that
you didn't do than by the ones you
did do. So throw off the bowlines.
Sail away from the safe harbor. Catch
the trade winds in your sails. Explore.
Dream. Discover.'

Mark Twain

'Whether you think you can or think you can't - you are right.'

Henry Ford

'I have discovered long since that it only needs a little courage to fulfil wishes which till then have been regarded as unobtainable'

Sigmund Freud

URI'S THREE GOLDEN MIND-POWER RULES

Number One: Focus!
Number Two: FOCUS!!
Number Three: FOCUS!!!

'The mind has exactly the same power as the hands: not merely to grasp the world, but to change it.'

Colin Wilson

'If you can fill the
unforgiving minute
With sixty seconds' worth
of distance run
Yours is the Earth
and everything that's in it'

Rudyard Kipling

'People are always blaming their circumstances for what they are. I don't believe in circumstances. The people who get on in the world are the people who get up and look for the circumstances they want and if they can't find them, make them.'

George Bernard Shaw

URI'S
TOP TEN
FEEL-GOOD PHRASES

I am a Winner.

I deserve to get
what I want.

I will wake up tomorrow
feeling **GREAT!**

No turning back!

That was then –
this is now.

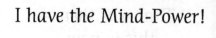

I have the Mind-Power!

◆

Yes, I can! Yes, I **WILL!**

I am doing this for me.
I love myself.
I deserve success.

I feel focused.

I am an Achiever. I get things done.

'Sometimes your joy is the source of your smile, but sometimes your smile can be the source of your joy.'

Thich Nhat Hanh

'Your vision will become clear only when you look into your heart. Who looks outside, dreams. Who looks inside, awakens.'

Carl Jung

---◆---

'A champion is afraid of losing –
everyone else is
afraid of winning.'

Billie Jean King

'The mind is not a vessel to be filled
but a fire to be kindled.'

Plutarch

---◆---

FAVOURITE MIND-POWER MUSIC
OR . . .
Using your ears to tune in your brain

Raid the bargain bins,
borrow from your public
library, and make your
Mind-Power unstoppable
– with rousing
pick-me-ups such as
**Elgar's Pomp And
Circumstance
March No.4**

When I am driving, I always keep to hand my complete antidote to road rage – a tape of Byron Janis playing **Chopin's Nocturnes**

To unblock your creativity, seize a blank sheet of paper and a pen, and scribble without pausing to think while you listen to **Rimsky-Korsakov's Scheherazade**

If my determination falters, and I need some steel in my soul, I crank up the hi-fi dial to 11 and rock out to anything
by
Pink Floyd

Amazing photographs by
Semyon Kirlian of the
electrical human aura have
revealed that math-
ematically precise music
creates patterns in our
energy field. To reorganise
a fragmented mind, try
**J.S.Bach's
Well-Tempered Klavier**

Home-sickness sometimes troubles me in faraway countries. I am transported in an instant to my Thames-side home by **Vaughan Williams's Fantasia On A Theme by Thomas Tallis**

———————◆———————

It is impossible to remain
depressed while listening
to the
**Benny Goodman
Orchestra**

———————◆———————

If you are angry with someone you love, practice forgiveness as you listen to **Soave Sia Il Vento** from **Mozart's Cosi Fan Tutte**

Imitate the single-minded determination and world-beating will-power that rings in every note of **Beethoven's Fifth Symphony**

Fantasise. Mind-Power is
a fantasy – if you can
dream it, you can do it.
I let my fantasies
run wild as I focus on
Holst's Planets

'We ask ourselves, 'Who am I to be brilliant, gorgeous, talented and fabulous?' Actually, who are you not to be? You are a child of God.'

Nelson Mandela after
Marianne Williamson

URI'S
TOP TEN
TECHNIQUES
TO RECHARGE
YOUR MIND-POWER

1
Make space to relax.
Stress can muffle your
inner voice.

2

Imagine yourself in a calm idyll. See it, smell it, breathe it. Dream it.

3

Make this idyll your
secret treat. Others can't
tell when you have flown
there.

4
Explore your idyll and let its beauty saturate you, so you are able to return to it in an instant.

5
Choose a piece of crystal
and hold it to your heart
- crystal amplifies human
energy.

6

Repeat these words three times in your calm idyll: 'My mind is filled with power.'

7

Repeat these words three
times in your calm idyll:
'I will achieve my target.'

8
Repeat these words three times in your calm idyll: 'I *will* succeed.'

9
Never let trespassers mock or belittle your idyll. It is yours and yours alone.

10

Return to your idyll and repeat your pledges frequently, until your Mind-Power shines and blazes. In this way you can achieve perfect peace of mind.

'People are just as happy as they
make up their minds to be.'

Abraham Lincoln

'Verily I say unto you, If ye have
faith as a grain of mustard seed, ye
shall say unto this mountain,
Remove hence to yonder place; and it
shall remove; *and nothing shall be
impossible unto you*.'

Matthew 17:20

'Imagination is more important
than knowledge.'

Albert Einstein

'The first and most important step
toward success is the feeling
that we can succeed.'

Nelson Boswell

MAKE YOUR BRAIN MORE POWERFUL THAN EINSTEIN'S

The greatest thinker of the 20th century said we used only 10 per cent of our brains. Read on to learn how he was wrong . . .

Our Mind-Power is like an iceberg, with 90 per cent lying hidden beneath the surface. Hidden, but still there. And awesomely massive.

We call the hidden 90 per cent of our Mind-Power the sub-conscious. The sub-conscious is like the sub-continent of Alexander's days – a vast treasure house, waiting to be explored and utilised.

Our sub-conscious is
always listening.
Listening, absorbing,
soaking up experience
like a sponge.
Talk to your sub-conscious.

Talk to the submerged 90 per cent of your mind. Tell it again and again:

I am strong.

I am relaxed.

I am happy.

Your sub-conscious will absorb this message, and make it true.

Sometimes your
sub-conscious talks back.
When it speaks, listen.

Messages from your
sub-conscious
are called
**Instincts. Intuitions.
Psychic gifts.**
Develop your psychic
Mind-Power – listen to
your sub-conscious.
And use even more of
your brain than Einstein.

URI'S FIVE FAVOURITE INSTANT MEDITATIONS

OR . . .

How to fly from where you are to where you want to be

Look up at the ultimate Millennium Dome - the night sky. Think how the light from uncountable million of stars has flowed across uncountable billions of light-years . . . directly to your own eyes.

Picture a river. Imagine your thoughts are like its waters. They flow through your head, swirl for a moment and are gone.
Let them go.

Breathe in deeply.
No-one need know.
You are simply breathing.
Count the breath. *One.*
Let it go. Breathe again.
Count two.
Let it go. Keep breathing.
Keep counting.
This is your secret
meditation.

—————— ◆ ——————

Go to a hospital. Stand
outside and look up at a
window. Whoever might be
inside - a child, a parent,
an old man or woman -
say a prayer that they will
be well soon. They need
your prayer more urgently
than you do.
**Because you are on the
outside of the hospital.**

—————— ◆ ——————

———————◆———————

Travel in time.
Look into your mind and
unlock a happy memory.
Something you have not
thought about in years.
Surprise yourself. Live this
memory. Revive the colours,
the smells, the textures.
Use every sense.
You have just travelled back
in time.

———————◆———————

'Great souls have wills, feeble ones
have only wishes.'

Chinese Proverb

'A man is happy so long as he
chooses to be happy and
nothing can stop him.'

Alexander Solzenitsyn

---◆---

'There is always a harmonious solution... if you stand back and give yourself time to find it.'

David Robertson

'This above all: *To thine own self be true*. And it must follow as the night the day, thou canst not then be false to any man.'

William Shakespeare

---◆---

URI'S
TOP TEN
HOME TRUTHS

There are no mistakes –
only lessons.

You can learn from
failure even more than
you can learn from
success.

---◆---

That isn't a barrier... it's a hurdle! You can leap it!

Your brain is a muscle –
give it some exercise

If you failed to get free
with a single bound, take
it step by step – but get
free anyway.

They can't beat you
unless you let them.

Putting things off is a
waste of energy. Be
decisive – act now.

Perfection is an excuse for failure. Don't hide behind the quest for perfection.

It is reassuring to fail,
and frightening to
succeed.
Face your fear.

---◆---

However tough the going
gets - the human mind
can be tougher.
Always be positive, be
optimistic.

---◆---

'Keep away from people who try to belittle your ambitions. Small people always do that, but the really great make you feel that you, too, can become great.'

Mark Twain

'It is not because things are difficult that we do not dare, it is because we do not dare that they are difficult.'

Seneca

◆

'The secret of health for both mind
and body is not to mourn for the
past, not to worry about the future,
not to anticipate troubles, but to live
in the present moment wisely and
earnestly.'

Buddha

'Time spent laughing is time spent
with the gods.'

Japanese Proverb

◆

'Life isn't about finding yourself. Life is about creating yourself.'

George Bernard Shaw

'Men do not live only by fighting evils. They live by positive goals... a vast variety of them.'

A.J. Ayer

'The one who says it cannot be done
should never interrupt the one
who is doing it.'

The Roman Rule

'It is funny about life: if you refuse to
accept anything but the very best you
will very often get it.'

W. Somerset Maugham

URI'S SENSATIONS:
SIX GIFTS
FROM THE GODS
Close Your Eyes
And Share
My Mind-Power
Fantasies . . .

———————◆———————

I am watching bright
sunlight turn an oily
patch of pollution on the
Thames to the fluorescent
purity of rainbows.

———————◆———————

I am listening to the burr
of a summer day, the
drone of the boats and
the flies and the distant,
murmuring words of
my companion.

I am inhaling the liquid sugar scent of roses, so deeply that the velvet petals turn to treacle on the back of my throat.

I am tasting the mouthful I have bitten from an apple - sharp as knowledge, crisp as truth, sweet as desire.

---◆---

I am touching the hair of
my wife and thrilling as
the silk threads glide
through my fingers like
electricity.

---◆---

I am aware I have been here before – the same experiences, the same emotions, the same day... but another life.

◆

'You can't have a better tomorrow if
you are thinking about yesterday all
the time.'

Charles F. Kettering

'A pessimist sees the difficulty in
every opportunity; an optimist sees
the opportunity in every difficulty.'

Sir Winston Churchill

◆

◆

'I find that the harder I work, the
more luck I seem to have.'

Thomas Jefferson

'Better to do something imperfectly
than to do nothing flawlessly.'

Robert Schuller

◆

'Nonfinishers sit around with other nonfinishers, and set up more discussions. Finishers know that to finish is worth a million conferences.'

Jeremy Baker

'Is not life a hundred times too short – to get bored?'

Friedrich Nietzsche

URI'S
TOP TEN MANTRAS
FOR GETTING
THINGS DONE

Do It *Now*

I Can and I Will

I know what I want

Lock on and hold on

Think Positive -
Think Yes

Never take No
for an answer

Quitters never win,
winners never quit

Excuses are for losers

---◆---

Everything is possible

Step by step, stay steady
on the target

———————————————— ◆ ————————————————

'There is nothing either good or bad,
but thinking makes it so.'

William Shakespeare

'God grant me the serenity to accept
the things I cannot change, the
courage to change the things I can
and the wisdom to distinguish the
one from the other.'

Traditional prayer

———————————————— ◆ ————————————————

'Act as if what you do makes a difference. It does.'

William James

'If there is no wind, row.'

Latin Proverb

'The journey of a thousand miles
must begin with a single step.'

Lao Tzu

'The future belongs to those who
believe in the beauty
of their dreams.'

Eleanor Roosevelt

'Laziness may appear attractive, but
work gives satisfaction.'

Anne Frank

'Satisfaction lies in the effort,
not in the attainment.
Full effort is full victory.'

Gandhi

URI'S TOP TEN SECRETS FOR BEATING SET-BACKS

Take the blame.
You must always accept
responsibility – to make
sure things don't go
wrong twice.

Take heart. Others have endured crueller set-backs than yours – and they still triumphed.

Take heed. This set-back can tell you what you're doing wrong – and how you can do it right.

Take a long, cool look.
Step outside yourself and
study the situation, like a
general surveying a map.

Be resilient. You need resilience to cope with the blow of each setback.

Be resourceful.
Resourcefulness will
create a strategy to beat
the set-back.

Be resolute. Your resolve
will carry the strategy to
victory.

Be patient. Set-backs
mean delays, but patience
will conquer.

Be persistent. Persistence will break down other people's objections and opposition.

Be perseverant. When one set-back follows another – perseverance will help you triumph.

'No one can make you feel inferior without your consent.'

Eleanor Roosevelt

'Mistakes are a fact of life. It is the response to the error that counts.'

Nikki Giovanni

'In order to cause a shadow to
disappear, you must shine
light on it.'

Shakti Gawain

'Whenever you fall,
pick something up.'

Oswald Avery

———————————◆———————————

'There is real magic in enthusiasm. It
spells the difference between
mediocrity and accomplishment.'

Norman Vincent Peale

'Obstacles are those frightful things
you see when you take your
eyes off your goals.'

Unknown

———————————◆———————————

URI'S
SEVEN ULTIMATE
INSPIRATIONS
People, Animals,
Ideas

---◆---

My wife, Hanna.

She is my anchor. My lodestone. **My heart.** She possesses the strength which sometimes I lack – to hold back my excesses.

---◆---

Brian Josephson.

His Nobel prize-winning work helped create microchip computers. **His mind never closes.** It is open to every conceivable idea.

---◆---

My four dogs.

They teach me the
imperative quality
of love . . .
**it must be
unconditional.**

---◆---

---◆---

The sixth astronaut
on the moon,
Captain Edgar Mitchell.
There is no challenge too
immense for man.
**There is no distance too
great for our minds to
travel.**

---◆---

MK Gandhi.

He sought spiritual purity, and **by seeking changed the world.** We can create anything, when we are prepared to create our better selves.

---◆---

Joan of Arc.
She heard the
voice of God.
We all of us hear the
voice of God. **But she
listened.**

---◆---

My imaginary
Buddhist monk.
He comes to me when I am
overwhelmed by
information. I picture him
in saffron robes, on a
snowy mountain peak. He
meditates for 24 hours at a
time, **his mind drifting**
far from the pollution
of mass media.

'To me, the definition of focus is knowing exactly where you want to be today, next week, next month, next year, then never deviating from your plan . . . You'll hit your target every time.'

Bruce Jenner

'A laser is a weak source of energy. A laser takes a few watts of energy and focuses them in a coherent stream of light. But with a laser, you can drill a hole in a diamond or wipe out cancer.'

Al Ries

---❖---

'The main thing is to keep the main
thing the main thing.'

Steven Covey

'The path to success is to take
massive, determined action.'

Anthony Robbins

---❖---

◆

'Patience, persistence and perspiration make an unbeatable combination for success.'

Napoleon Hill

'Lord, grant that I may always desire more than I accomplish.'

Michelangelo

'Success is the child of audacity.'

Benjamin Disraeli

◆

URI'S
TOP TEN PROMISES
WE CAN MAKE
TO OURSELVES

I will complete, I will
finish, I will see it
through.
I will make it.

I've come this far – I won't let anything or anyone stop me now.

Cynicism is for cowards.
I am brave.

I deserve the best. I will demand the best. I will settle for nothing less.

---◆---

This is my life, and I will
live up to it.

---◆---

---◆---

If I fail I will forgive
myself - and always
believe I can succeed
again.

---◆---

I will not hide behind
excuses.

I will do my best
and be proud of it.

I have made up my mind
– no-one can unmake it.

When I achieve my target
I will allow myself to
rejoice.

'The most beautiful thing we can experience is the mysterious. It is the source of all true art and science.'

Albert Einstein

'The mind, like the universe, is ever expanding. And the mind, like the universe, has no limits.'

Byron Janis

---◆---

'Become light. Go beyond the
consciousness of your own physical
body and you will remain ever
healthy, wealthy
and happy.'

Dadi Janki

'Don't forget to love yourself.'

Soren Kierkegaard

---◆---

Focus on this angel for one minute.
Say a prayer in your heart
for someone in need.

Concentrate on this shape
for 60 seconds.
Send your positive, healing energy
and your pure love
to somebody, anywhere in the world,
who needs it most.

Focus on this symbol for 30 seconds
and make a singular wish.
Repeat three times:

'It will come true.'
'It will come true.'
'It will come true.'

Remember always -
Be positive
Be optimistic
Stay hopeful
Have faith

I wish you health, happiness
and peace of mind.

Uri Geller

Mind-Colour Powers

(1) Tune in to Green for meditation – it's the colour of Mind-Power calm.

(2) Focus on Orange for energy – the spectrum's most vibrant shade.

(3) Be positive with Yellow – this colour is bursting with good vibrations.

(4) Heal yourself with Blue – it stimulates natural antiseptics and activates the immune system.

(5) Contact your sub-conscious with Violet – the truly psychic shade.

(6) Energise your Mind-Power with Red – it stokes up your adrenalin.

I have sealed a secret drawing in my safe.
At 11am and 11pm GMT, on the 11th
of each month, I will transmit the
drawing telepathically. During the total
eclipse of the sun at 11 minutes past 11
on August 11, 1999, I will open the
envelope. The drawing will be
revealed on my website at
http://www.urigeller.com
Send me your drawings, at
Robson Books Ltd, Bolsover House,
5-6 Clipstone Street, London W1P 8LE,
United Kingdom. The one which most
closely matches mine will win a valuable
rock crystal, millions of years old,
from my collection.